HOW TO MASTER

Financial
Freedom

A Proven Series of Principles
to Budget Your Expenses,
Manage Your Income, Invest in
Real Estate and the Stock Market,
and Achieve Financial Freedom

ARDI AAZIZNIA

© Ardi Aaziznia
Chief Risk Manager and Investment Analyst
Peak Capital Trading
www.PeakCapitalTrading.com

Contents

AUTHOR'S REMARKS

I recently googled the words "financial freedom," and the search came up with 798,000,000 results. A search of Amazon.com with "financial freedom book" yielded over 2,000 results.

Among those many books were several popular classics, including one of my favorites, Robert Kiyosaki's mega-selling 13-book series, *Rich Dad, Poor Dad*. The original was first published in 1997, and Amazon listed others whose publication also spanned several decades.

Since there are already so many books to choose from, why would you want to read mine?

First, this is a current book (2020). It draws on proven strategies that have been possible only in the last few years, thanks to technological advancement.

Secondly, it pays particular attention to Generation Y and Generation Z readers. That's not to say that older people won't find the book useful, but relatively little has been published on the subject that Millennials and Gen Y people can relate to. And this is one of very few that have an author who can be classified as late millennial and not far removed from the Gen Z cut-off.

My goal is for this book to be informative and useful without including lots of personal details, so you won't be reading anecdotes about my early experiences and my career path. While you might (or more likely might not) enjoy such stories, I doubt that they would be all that relevant to your goal of financial freedom. Plus, to be perfectly honest, I'm too young to reminisce.

I decided to write this book to help the people from my generation achieve their financial goals and not fall into financial traps that might take years to escape. You might ask why you should listen to me. Well, my background is in finance, and I graduated from one of the top universities in Canada. I am a certified Financial Modeling and Valuation Analyst and have worked in venture capital and private wealth management for the last several years. I am currently the head of the risk department for Peak Capital Trading, a proprietary trading firm in Vancouver. My background working in the wealth management industry has allowed me to observe many clients' behaviours and learn some of the key habits of wealthier individuals. I have summarized my experience in this industry into ten easy to follow rules to help anyone get started on their path to financial freedom.

Truth be told, you do not need advanced education in economics or business to be financially savvy. My experience has allowed me to understand the key features that make a difference in an individual's personal net worth even when their actual income remains unchanged. Whether it is taking advantage of the tax code, investing, or creating budgets, the secret to generating long-term wealth is far more than just increasing your income. My goal is to help you not only make more money but also save and effectively invest your money. Remember that financial literacy is a journey and not a destination. No matter your income, your investment portfolio, or your spending habits, there are always more tricks and strategies to learn and areas where you can constantly improve. As a finance professional, I practice what I advocate and try to expand my knowledge every day.

To me, financial freedom means being smart with money. I am not trying to sell you the idea of a two-day work week or working remotely by the beach (although this is what you see everyday on YouTube advertisements). I see myself as financially free, despite working 60 to 70 hours a week, because I can make decisions that will yield me the highest return and liberate me from being dependent on others.

Finally, I wrote this book on the assumption that its readers are relative novices in the financial field and that using a lot of technical language is unnecessary.

In order to make this book easier to digest, I decided to break it down into three main categories. The first part teaches you how to increase your income. After all, if you are not making enough, it is hard to become financially independent. The second part is designed to help you manage your income better, whether it is taking advantage of tax code or using new applications that help you budget better. The first two parts of the book will help you collectively increase your savings. And last but not least, the final section shows you some key strategies for investing your savings and helping you slowly grow your money and reach financial dependence. You can see the breakdown of this book in the figure below:

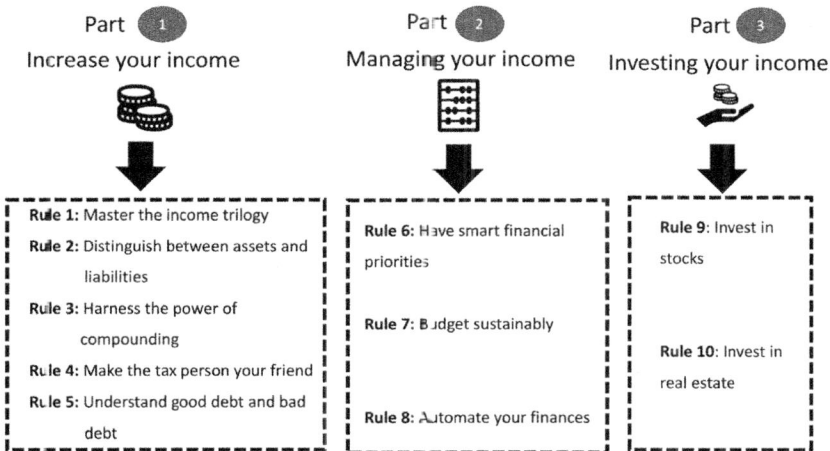

Part 1	Part 2	Part 3
Increase your income	Managing your income	Investing your income
Rule 1: Master the income trilogy	**Rule 6:** Have smart financial priorities	**Rule 9:** Invest in stocks
Rule 2: Distinguish between assets and liabilities		
Rule 3: Harness the power of compounding	**Rule 7:** Budget sustainably	
Rule 4: Make the tax person your friend		**Rule 10:** Invest in real estate
Rule 5: Understand good debt and bad debt	**Rule 8:** Automate your finances	

Figure x: A breakdown of how this book is divided. In the first portion, I show you some ways to increase your income. In the second part, I discuss how to manage your increased income. The last part is devoted to helping you invest your additional income.

This book marks my second venture into sharing some of the knowledge I have gained over the last few years while working and studying. Recently, I worked alongside veteran day trader Andrew Aziz to write a comprehensive book on trading and investing: Stock Market Explained: A Beginners Guide to Investing and Trading in the Modern Stock Market. If, after reading this book, you are curious to learn more about the capital markets, feel free to check that publication out.

I'd really like to hear from you with questions, comments, criticisms, and suggestions for updating and revising this book, and, if all goes well, maybe even some ideas for more books that would make this the first in a series. Please feel free to reach out to me at *Ardi@peakcapitaltrading.com*. I hope you enjoy this book.

Ardi Aaziznia, FMVA

INTRODUCTION: YOUR PATH TO FINANCIAL FREEDOM

Living Paycheck to Paycheck

Merriam-Webster explains that "to live paycheck to paycheck" means "to spend all of the money from one paycheck before receiving the next paycheck."[1]

A 2017 CareerBuilder survey revealed that 78% of workers in the U.S. lived from paycheck to paycheck, just managing to pay their bills, and that almost one in ten workers with incomes over $100,000 also lived with these same limitations. Now, this might come to you as a surprise and lead you to wonder how an individual making over $100,000 could possibly be living from paycheck to paycheck. The answer is simply because your financial health has nothing to do with how much you are making.

Let me break this down using a business example. Take Uber (ticker:UBER) as an example. The company has been public since May 2019 and is a household name in the business of transportation. Uber's 2019 revenue was over $14 billion, and yet it reported a net loss of over $8 billion (see statement below). Although losing money was a strategic move to gain market share, this example simply illustrates that if you are not monitoring your spending, you're more likely to go under. To this day, there are many public companies that are losing billions every quarter despite making billions.

---

1   Merriam-Webster, s. v. "live paycheck to paycheck," accessed October 30, 2020, https://www.merriam-webster.com/dictionary/live%20paycheck%20to%20paycheck

	Year Ended December 31,				
	2015[1]	2016[1]	2017	2018	2019
	(Unaudited)				
	(In millions, except share amounts which are reflected in thousands, and per share amounts)				
Consolidated Statements of Operations Data:					
Revenue	$ 1,995	$ 3,845	$ 7,932	$ 11,270	$ 14,147
Total costs and expenses[2]	3,334	6,868	12,012	14,303	22,743
Loss from operations	(1,339)	(3,023)	(4,080)	(3,033)	(8,596)
Income (loss) from continuing operations before income taxes and loss from equity method investment[3]	(1,603)	(3,218)	(4,575)	1,312	(8,433)
Income (loss) from discontinued operations, net of income taxes[4]	(1,098)	2,876	—	—	—
Net income (loss) attributable to Uber Technologies, Inc.	(2,688)	(370)	(4,033)	997	(8,506)

Figure 1: Snapshot of Uber income statement. Uber lost over 8 billion in 2019 despite having revenues of over 14 billion. This represents that regardless of how much you make, if you can not control your spending, you will lose money.

A more recent (2020) Willis Towers Watson Global Benefits Attitudes Survey of 8,000 American workers found 38% living paycheck to paycheck and 39% who would not be able to come up with $3,000 if an emergency arose.

These rather startling statistics could be taken at first glance to indicate insufficient income to meet reasonable month-to-month family living expenses. The inclusion of large numbers of people making over $100,000, however, suggests that the reason for running out of money every month is not something so obvious.

The root cause of this widespread problem is one of the issues this book will explore.

The onset of the horrific 2020 pandemic that led to millions of cases of COVID-19 and hundreds of thousands of deaths around the world forced previously-inconceivable lockdowns, travel restrictions, and the closure of countless businesses, some temporarily but many permanently. Job losses in the U.S. from mid-March to the end of April totaled 20.6 million and resulted in an unemployment rate of 14.7%, a grim statistic that was comparable to the Great Depression of the 1930s. The total number of lost jobs more than doubled what occurred during the Great Recession of 2007-2009, when 8.7 million Americans found themselves jobless.

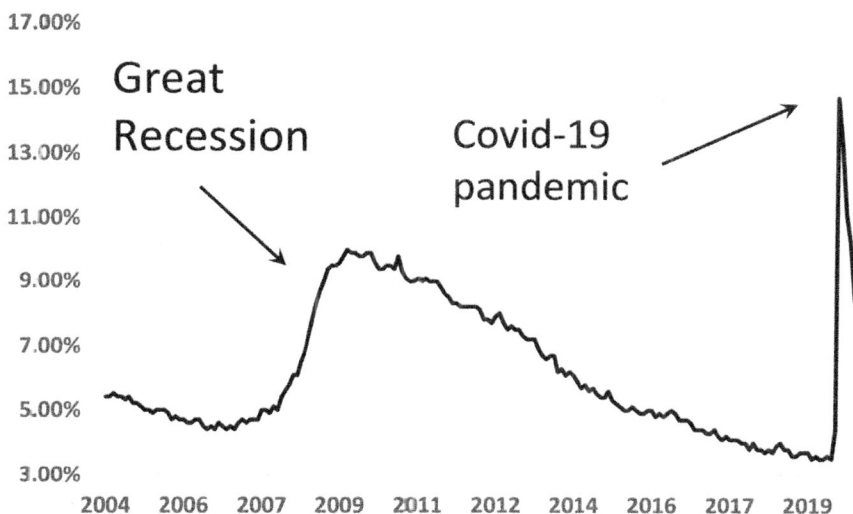

Great
Recession

Covid-19
pandemic

17.00%
15.00%
13.00%
11.00%
9.00%
7.00%
5.00%
3.00%

2004 2006 2007 2009 2011 2012 2014 2016 2017 2019

Figure 2: U.S. unemployment hit the highest levels on record during the pandemic of 2020. During these times, individuals, more than ever, needed to be smart with their money.

Such unprecedented and unforeseeable developments undoubtedly caused considerable hardship for even the best-prepared families and individuals. But to suddenly be without a job for months on end or to have reliable sources of income simply disappear would have been especially difficult for those who had not set aside adequate emergency funds to help tide them over until they could return to their jobs or find new ones.

Not surprisingly, during this time, more and more people became interested in the stock market. Looking at the google search trend, you will see a surge in searches for "stock market" around the same time lockdowns were imposed. Is it because people lost their jobs and were looking for a chance to recover some of their lost income in the market?

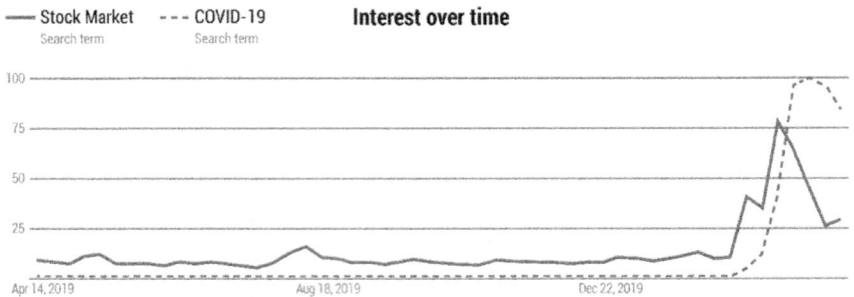

Figure 3: "COVID-19" and "Stock Market" keyword Google search trends between April 2019 and April 2020. As you can see, there is a clear correlation. As the stock market drop hit the news cycles, people started searching more and more about the stock market on Google!

Hopefully, by the time you are reading this, a vaccine has eradicated COVID-19, but we can be assured that another catastrophe of some sort will appear at some point in the future. If there were ever convincing arguments for having room for movement in personal budgets and for having enough emergency funds set aside to pay the bills for at least several months, COVID-19 provided them. There's no doubt that "be prepared for the unexpected" was one of the most powerful messages delivered by the pandemic.

Acquiring Financial Literacy

You have probably heard the term "financial literacy" over and over again. But what does it really mean? Being financially literate means having the knowledge and skills to make intelligent decisions about financial matters. It includes possessing a good working knowledge of the basic principles of business and finance.

Financial literacy is one of the most important life skills a person can develop, but unfortunately, it is not something that has generally been emphasized in schools. Fortunately, school systems have recently been including this concept in their curricula; plus, there is now quite a bit of useful information available through classes, books, online sources like podcasts and blogs, and lots and lots of googling. All of these can help people increase their financial intelligence.

What is it so important about financial literacy? One major reason is that it helps individuals understand which decisions are most likely to help them achieve their financial goals and to have the ability to carry out those decisions effectively.

Studying Typical Income and Expenditure Figures

According to the U.S. Bureau of Labor Statistics, consumers in 2018 made $67,421 annually after taxes on average and spent $61,224. That spending worked out to $5,102 each month for the average American household. It broke down as follows:

- 32. 8% ($1,674) for housing

- 15.9% ($813) for transportation (including public transit, lease or loans payments, fuel and servicing)

- 11.9% ($608) for personal insurance and pensions

- 8.1% ($414) for health care

- 7.3% ($372) for groceries

- 5.6% ($288) for restaurants

- 5.3% ($269) for entertainment

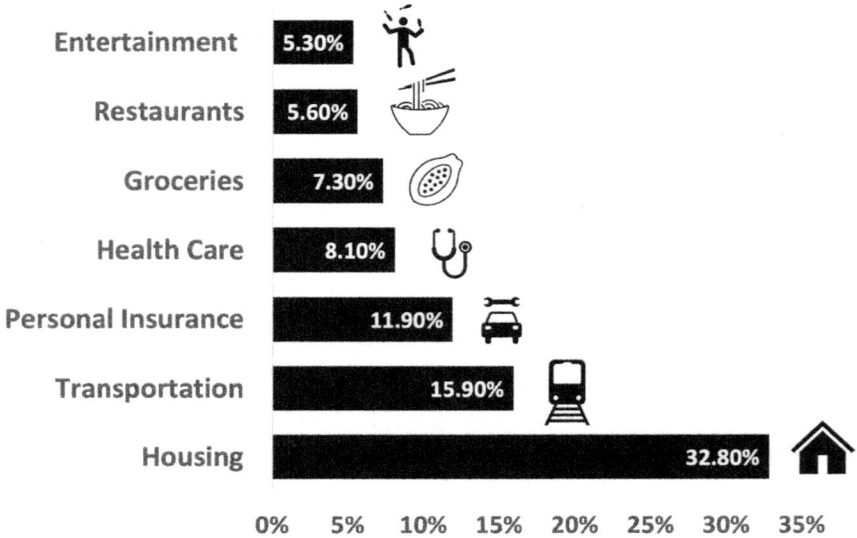

Category	Percentage
Entertainment	5.30%
Restaurants	5.60%
Groceries	7.30%
Health Care	8.10%
Personal Insurance	11.90%
Transportation	15.90%
Housing	32.80%

0%   5%   10%   15%   20%   25%   30%   35%

Figure 4: Average American household spending breakdown. Housing and transportation account for more than 50% of household spending.

Other categories at around 3% or less included cash contributions, apparel and related services, education, and personal care. These survey results do not include any indication of how much of average annual surplus of $6,197 went into savings or investments.

Looking Ahead to Retirement

Many people underestimate the amount of money they need to save so they can live comfortably during their retirement years. Thanks to medical advancements, as well as better nutritional and lifestyle habits, people now live much longer and therefore need more money than ever to retire. Since 1900, the global average life expectancy has more than doubled and is now approximately 80 years.

Many people are unsure about how much money they will need to retire comfortably, and, if anything, they tend to underestimate it. The Benchmark Chart below provides an easy-to-visualize way to clarify that issue. Assuming that a person plans to retire at age 65 and will need a reserve of funds for the following 20 or 30 years, this table shows their age (on the left side) and the multiples of their annual salary they will need to have saved by that age (on the right side).

Benchmark Chart

Age	Saved
35	2x
40	3x
45	4x
50	5x
55	6x
60	7x
65	8x

Figure 5: The above chart shows how much you need to have saved to retire comfortably at 65. As an example, by 35, you should have saved twice your salary.

Let's look at the amount you need to be saving from a different angle. Not only is *when* you start saving important but also *how* you save your money. Imagine starting at 25 years old and planning to retire at 65. You have 40 years to save, and your goal is to put aside a reasonable amount of $500 per month. Another question becomes what do you need to invest your money in? Should you put your money under a mattress or save it in a zero-interest checking account? Should you put it in a risk-free saving account? In the market? Or in real estate?

Your choice of investment vehicle can directly impact how well you can retire, and this is why financial literacy matters the most. Different asset classes have different rates of return. The money you put under your mattress or keep in the bank with no interest is actually losing you 2–3% due to inflation. Your home gains the value of 4%, and the stock market gets you somewhere from 5–7% annually. The risk-free saving rate is about 1% annually. Of course, these are all averages based on historical returns and these numbers are not guaranteed. But this is a great measure to demonstrate that your choices will impact how well you will retire.

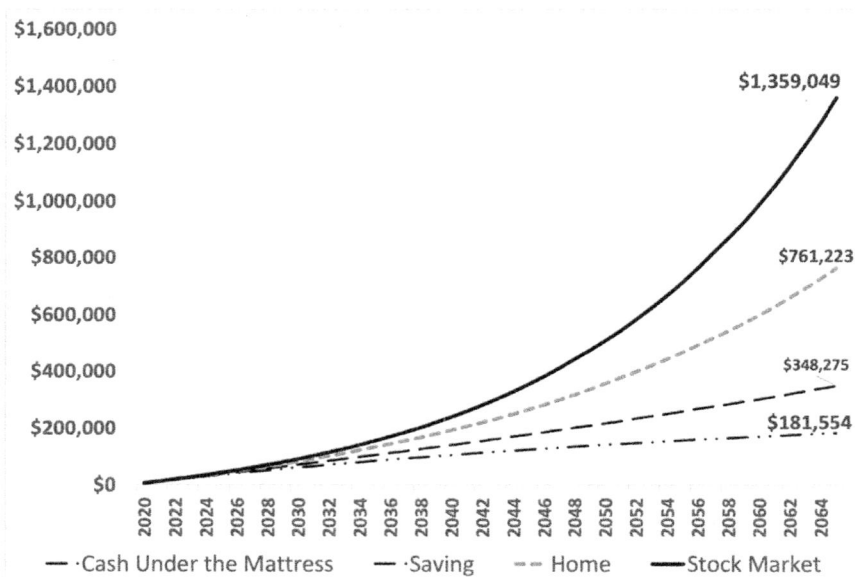

Figure 6: Different rates of return can make a huge impact on your retirement in the long run. Saving $500 a month in different asset classes with different returns can make a huge difference over the long term.

If you find yourself occasionally wondering if you should be doing more about your long-term financial needs (including providing for your retirement years), do not be too hard on yourself. First of all, a bit of wondering and worrying about saving is a good first step towards actually doing something. Secondly, you are not alone. There are all kinds of people just like you who understand that everyone in general should start making financial arrangements for their retirement well before they reach that stage in their lives, but somehow, they just don't seem to get around to taking action.

Psychologists have conducted some interesting studies to try to understand why so many people tend not to be very good at long-range planning. One conclusion they have reached is that many of us tend to regard our future selves as strangers rather than as an older (and hopefully wiser) version of our current selves. The researchers found that the more a person sees their future self as remote and different from themself at the present time, the more likely they are to procrastinate in dealing with such long-range plans as saving for retirement, as well as more immediate goals like eating better or exercising more.

People who are able to visualize themselves in the future as being essentially the same person they are today have been shown to be more capable of planning better for the future. They don't put off making these kinds of plans on the assumption that somehow the passage of time will turn them into a completely different person who will somehow have the skills, time, and resources to engage in activities that they are just not prepared to do today.

Some psychologists have tried to help people become more realistic in visualizing themselves later in their lives by having them create their own personal timelines. Other psychologists (as well as investment firms) have even encouraged clients to try out computer programs that digitally age still photos of themselves on the assumption that seeing their own greying. balding, wrinkling images will drive home the reality that they will indeed get old.

Now that we have established why it is important to start saving money for retirement and developed some understanding of why we are so bad at saving, let's take on the journey of financial literacy to help us achieve our financial goals.

PART 1

🔑 INCREASING YOUR INCOME

RULE 1

Master the Income Trilogy

If you do not find a way to make money while you sleep, you will work until you die.
— **Warren Buffett**

Three Types of Income

In order to get on top of your finances, you need to first understand what income really means and what the different types of income are. When most people hear the term "personal income," their first thought is about the money that appears in their bank accounts every pay period for doing whatever work they are paid to do. This is generally referred to as "earned income." But there are actually three main categories of income. While earned income is the most common and most attainable, your goal should be to have all three types of income in order to enjoy genuine financial freedom. Here is a bit of information about the three types of income:

1. Earned income: This is what you earn in your job (or jobs) and, incidentally, where you pay the highest percentage in income tax. Your goal should be to save and invest in a way that the cashflow earned from this type of income becomes less essential to your lifestyle. In your 20s and 30s, most of your cashflow would probably come from this type of income, but as you save, invest, and make smart decisions, this type of income should become less significant and eventually be completely phased out. While I do recommend you leave this stage as quickly as possible, it is helpful to increase this income as much as possible while you are in the early stages of your career.

It can be beneficial to think of your personal finances in much the same way that businesses view their own financial situations. The number one goal of businesses is to maximize their revenues or gross sales in order to succeed. Similarly, any legitimate steps you can take to increase your own income can make a big difference to your financial and personal success. Even if the pay from your regular job is sufficient to meet your everyday needs and perhaps provide some extra for saving and investments, having additional sources of earned income can open more doors of opportunity to reach your long-term goals.

One way to do this is to take advantage of the gig economy, which involves temporary, flexible, or freelance jobs. Some of the best-known examples are using your own vehicle to drive for Uber or Lyft, or to deliver restaurant meals for Doordash or GrubHub. Online classified sites like Craigslist list available gigs as well as postings from jobseekers. Fiverr, which features pricing in multiples of $5, gives gig seekers opportunities to offer their online services around the world.

Let me break this down further with a personal story. During my first year out of school, I had a full-time job plus two part time gigs to help me with my finances. I was working my regular 50–60-hours-per-week finance job (yes, we put in long hours in finance, but I can't complain because I love my job) in addition to being a teacher assistant at the University of British Columbia and writing finance-related articles for various websites.

I had a strict goal of saving $3,000 a month, which I planned to invest in the portfolio of stocks and bonds that I had constructed using the techniques I had learned from school and work. (I share some of these techniques with you as part of Rule 9 and Rule 10 in the coming chapters). If you add the time I was studying for my CFA, and other online education, I was working around the clock, but I knew that was the price I had to pay to reach my goals.

Now, I know financial freedom differs from person to person and I wish I had an easier option for you, but the truth is, you have to work hard and increase your earned income in order to be able to generate the other two types of income. I wish I could tell you there is an "online drop shipping course" that will make you wealthy and generate passive income, but while the internet has made making additional income much easier, the principles are still the same, and it starts with hard work. I do not shy away from telling you that I work long hours, but I do also enjoy the occasional notification on my phone that says a certain amount of dividend has been deposited to my account.

There are many ways to maximize the spending power of all your types of income through planning and budgeting strategies, and these will be discussed under Rule 7.

2. Capital gain income: Capital gains are profits made on assets (the difference between the purchase price and the selling price). Capital assets can include homes ("flipping" houses), investment properties, stocks, bonds, and collectibles such as art. In the U.S., short-term capital gains (less than one year) are taxed at the same rate as ordinary income. Long-term capital gains (more than one year) are taxed at lower rates.

Try thinking of capital gain income as the fruits of your labor. Increasing your earned income allows you to start investing, and investing will let you take advantage of capital gain income. As I am writing this book in May of 2020, my portfolio is up 7.73% for the year. This is an unrealized capital gain, since I still have not sold my stocks. In the event that I sell and liquidate my portfolio, 50% of my capital gain would be taxed at the appropriate tax rate. While tax laws differ from country to country, taxes on capital gains are generally much lower than taxes on employment.

3. Passive income: As the name suggests, passive income refers to earnings acquired from an enterprise in which a person is not directly involved. This can include rental properties and limited partnerships. This income can generate cash flow and is generally taxed at a lower rate.

Many of us have dreamed of actually having passive income. The reality is that passive income is possible and can be rewarding, but in order to get to this step, you first need to master the other two types of income. Some examples of passive income are earnings from rental real estate or dividends of stocks you have invested in. There are many companies with strong balance sheets and which offer attractive annual dividends of 6–8%. This means that an investment of $100,000 would guarantee $8,000 in annual income. This is in addition to potential capital gains from the stock. And, as an added bonus, dividends are usually taxed at relatively low rates since the corporations issuing them have already paid large amounts in taxes.

Another example is real estate investing. While many people assume that this would require having thousands in savings and multiple properties, you can actually start with a spare bedroom or an unused basement. Websites like Airbnb have changed the real estate game completely, and now anyone can start generating consistent income by utilizing this popular method. A few of my clients are paying off the mortgages on their vacation homes solely by renting them out for a few months of the year.

The Cash Flow Quadrant

In his second book, Rich Dad's Cashflow Quadrant (1998), Robert Kiyosaki explained this now-famous concept in detail. Although legal considerations (and respect for Robert Kiyosaki) prevent us from publishing his trademarked drawing of the quadrant, we will describe the concept as clearly as we can.

First, please imagine four squares or rectangles, with two on the left (one on top of the other) and two on the right in the same arrangement. The top left side of the quadrant is marked with an "E," which stands for employees. These are people who work for a company or an organization and are dependent on such companies for their livelihood. Most of their waking hours are spent doing that work, and if they lose their job or their employer closes down, they will lose that income and probably have serious financial difficulties. Kiyosaki explains that employees value security highly and avoid taking risks.

The bottom left quarter ("S") represents self-employed people (which includes small business owners and professional specialists). As the name suggests, people in quadrant two work for themselves. They are generally in a more secure situation than employees, but they are dependent on the continuing loyalty of their customers and clients and can be in serious trouble if demand for their products or services declines or if there is a downturn in the economy. Their taxes are generally relatively high.

In the third quadrant on the top right side ("B") are business owners (with 500+ employees) who are willing to hire people with specialized skills and to delegate responsibilities. They continue, however, to maintain control of their businesses. Business owners have some definite advantages: they can control production, hire employees, and find creative ways to pay taxes, such as writing off business expenses and taking advantage of changes in the economy.

The fourth quadrant on the bottom right ("I") represents investors. This is the place to be! Investors concentrate on finding assets (often using other people's money) that will generate cash flow. Income from those assets enables them to acquire even more assets, such as real estate, savings, bonds, and sources of dividends. According to Kiyosaki, investors are the richest people in the world, don't have to work unless they want to, and have the highest level of financial security. They also have the most tax breaks.

The *Rich Dad, Poor Dad* philosophy encourages all people, including employees in quadrant one, to move to quadrant four by becoming investors. Kiyosaki maintains that everyone can save money and find their way to financial freedom.

A basic purpose of my book is to provide you with information so you too can move from quadrant one to quadrant four and enjoy the many benefits of financial independence.

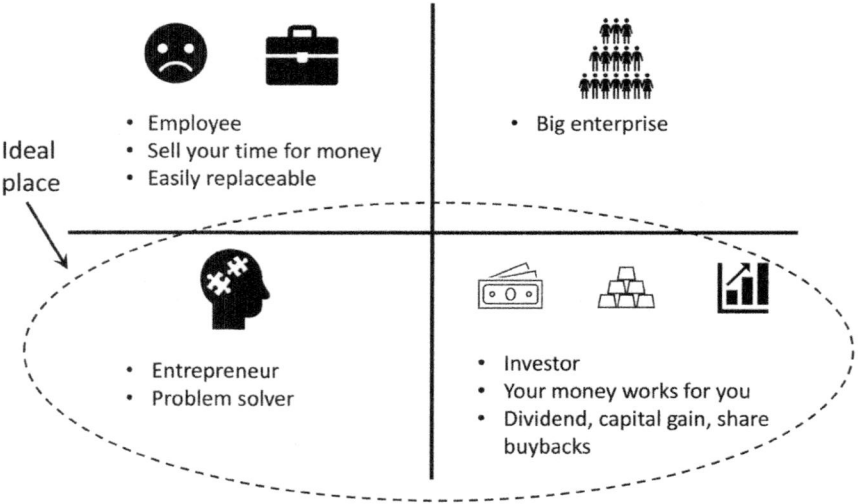

Figure 7: Visual representation of what the four quadrants might look like. The key is that in the top two quadrants, you are trading your time and skill for money. Almost everyone starts in the top two quadrants. Ideally, as life goes on, you move into the bottom two quadrants.

RULE 2

Distinguish Between Assets and Liabilities

Liabilities Are Not Assets

For families and individuals, assets have traditionally been defined as what you own, such as a house, a car, furniture, and clothing. Liabilities have been defined as what you owe, such as outstanding loans, mortgages, and credit card balances. The difference between these two has been referred to as your net worth.

But let's take a moment to think about these examples. For previous generations, ownership of the family home was regarded as one of the best examples of an asset, as well as being a very good investment. This widely held belief was based on the assumption that a house or condo would increase in value over a number of years and could be resold at a profit. Many families proudly passed on stories of members of previous generations who had bought houses, raised their families in them for decades, and when the nests became empty and the owners no longer had the interest or the energy to maintain them, easily sold them for many times the original purchase price. If you recall, however, from Figure 6, there are other investment opportunities that a provide better rate of return than owning a home.

One factor that is often ignored when relating these stories is the amount of money that was spent over those decades on taxes, maintenance, and repairs. Of course, these expenses can be counterbalanced to at least some extent by the value of having lived in the home. Another even more important factor is inflation. A number of studies have concluded that over the decades, housing values in the U.S. have actually increased by little more than the rate of inflation.

Can we assume that this apparent and perhaps illusory pattern of increases in housing prices will continue? The average sale price of homes in the U.S. steadily increased from 1963–2007, and many Americans believed that this trend would continue indefinitely. Then the housing bubble popped, and the financial crisis of 2008 emerged. After housing prices peaked in early 2006, they began moving downward over the next year or two until reaching new lows in 2012.

By 2013, the average sales price of homes sold in the U.S. bounced back to pre-2008 levels, and the historic trend of steady increases in housing prices appeared to re-establish itself until 2018. That year, the prices flattened, and then, in 2019, began to gradually decline. These trends and the actual percentages, of course, varied from one part of the country to another.

Sudden and dramatic changes in the housing market and in sale prices have frequently been caused by unanticipated economic developments. One of the early results of the 2020 coronavirus pandemic, for instance, was a recession that saw a drop in home prices. With so many businesses closing and so many people at least temporarily unemployed, uncertainty prevailed and very few people were willing to consider buying a home. Purchase contracts were scarce because of mortgage difficulties, shutdowns and social distancing made home showings challenging, and business closures made realtors and appraisers unavailable.

Although the housing market has historically rebounded from a variety of crises, the point can certainly be made that the kind of virtually guaranteed increases in housing values that prevailed during the twentieth century and a few years beyond can no longer be depended on. The certainty of our grandparents and parents that their homes would appreciate over the years is not something we can embrace.

We also need to question the commonly held belief that home ownership is a form of investment. There are several reasons this is not necessarily valid. One major difference between a home and an investment is that the main purpose of a home is to provide accommodation, while the fundamental goal of an investment is to generate profit. The owner has control over when to sell an investment, and that is usually done when it will result in the best return. The decision to sell a home, on the other hand, is usually based on family and individual lifestyle changes, and those don't necessarily coincide with optimum housing prices.

A second consideration is that even though houses generally increase in value, the owner is usually able to benefit from that increase in only one way: by selling it. That entails having to move out, with all of the inconveniences and expenses that go with moving. And when a home is sold, in most cases the equity will be needed to buy another home — at current prices. This means that the home equity is actually trapped equity.

Finally, as mentioned earlier, there are ongoing costs ("carrying costs") associated with homes, including mortgage payments, taxes, insurance, repairs, maintenance, and remodeling. Such ongoing costs are not generally involved with investments.

And then there are other kinds of liabilities that are sometimes perceived as assets. A car that you lease or own is anything but an asset considering that the average new car begins to depreciate the moment it leaves the dealership and can lose almost 40% of its value in its first three years. Buying used, or not having a car at all, might make more financial sense. Because possessions like furniture or clothing have little or no resale value, these definitely cannot be considered assets.

Cash Is King

Merriam-Webster defines cash flow as "a flow of cash; especially one that provides solvency."[1]

In the opinion of many financial experts, true assets must generate cash flow. Unlike a capital gain, which is a one-time benefit for the profit that results from the sale of an investment, cash flow is the gift to yourself that keeps on giving. Often paid on a monthly, quarterly, or annual basis, cash flow continues in an ongoing pattern. And unlike a capital gain, where the asset must be sold to realize profit, cash flow gives investors the best of both worlds: steady income while still retaining ownership. On Wall Street, analysts value companies based on cash flow. As part of my job, I conduct discount cash flow models (forecasting a company's future cashflows and discounting them back to the present) to determine if a certain investment is right for my client.

In some circumstances, a liability can actually become an asset. For instance, while a homeowner simply lives in the home and makes the mortgage payments hoping that its value will eventually increase, that home is a liability because it is taking cash from the owner's pockets. But if that same homeowner decides to move out to live with friends or family members or to rent an inexpensive apartment and then rent out the entire house (or even decides to stay there but rent out rooms) the house will become an asset because it is putting cash into the owner's pockets.

---

1 *Merriam-Webster, s. v.* "cash flow," accessed October 30, 2020, https://www.merriam-webster.com/dictionary/cash%20flow

RULE 3

Harness the Power of Compounding

"Compound interest is the eighth wonder of the world. He who understands it, earns it... he who doesn't... pays it."—**Albert Einstein**

Start Early

When is the best time for you to start investing? The one-word answer to that question is "now." Regardless of the age or stage of life you are in, start investing now. There is no such time as too early, and fortunately, there is no such time as too late. And it doesn't matter all that much how much you invest to start with. A few dollars would be acceptable; more than a few dollars would be better.

Why should you start investing now? The two-word answer to that question is "compound interest."

The Compounding Effect

Compound interest has often been compared to a snowball rolling down a hill. The more it rolls, the more snow it accumulates and the larger it becomes. That's how compound interest works. It's fine to earn some interest on the principal you deposit, but it's much better to keep earning interest on the interest you have already earned. The interest you earn keeps compounding itself, and it doesn't take long for the interest that has been accumulated to be a larger amount then the original deposit you made.

A Tale of Two Brothers

Here's an example of how compound interest can work. Imagine two brothers. One is 30 years old and the other is 40, and each decides to invest $10,000 a year until he reaches the retirement age of 65.

As the table below shows, the older brother will have just short of $1,444,164 when he retires. His younger sibling will have a much more promising pool of money that's more than $1 million larger than his brother's retirement fund.

Why is there such a big difference? Well, certainly the younger brother had an extra ten years to make deposits, and that works out to $100,000. But what really accounts for the more than a million-dollar difference in their final figures is the extra ten years of compounding (at an average return rate of 9%, which is normal for stock market). Much of that difference is due to the interest-upon-interest advantage of having an earlier start.

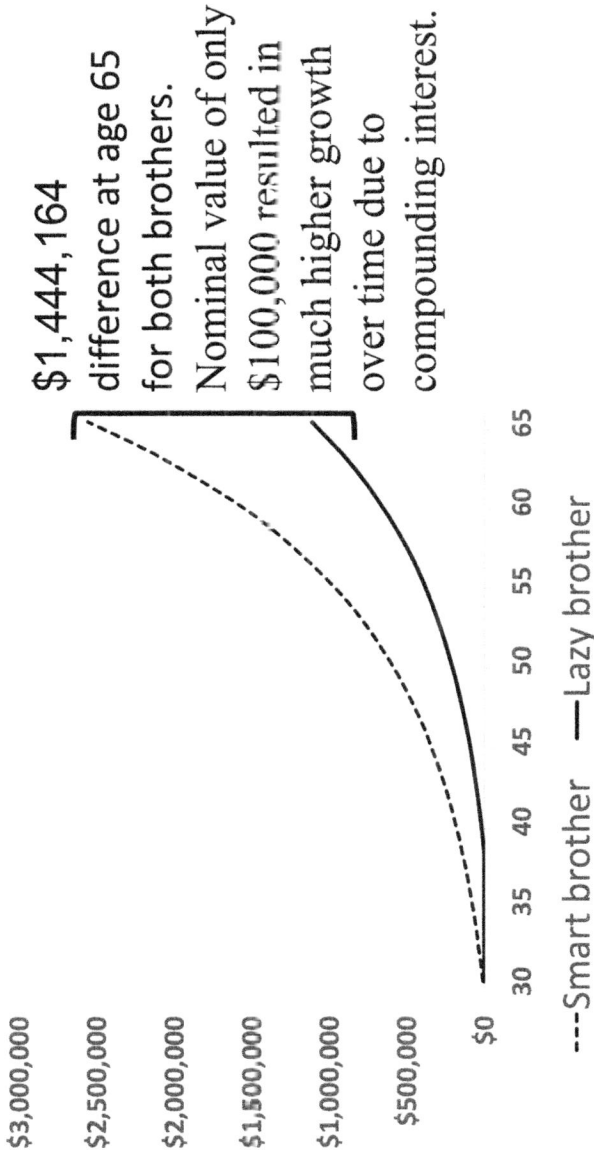

$1,444,164 difference at age 65 for both brothers. Nominal value of only $100,000 resulted in much higher growth over time due to compounding interest.

--- Smart brother   —— Lazy brother

$3,000,000
$2,500,000
$2,000,000
$1,500,000
$1,000,000
$500,000
$0

30 35 40 45 50 55 60 65

Figure 8: Although the younger brother only starts ten years earlier than the older brother, after 35 years, due to compounding, the difference is over $1,400,000. I used 9% compound rate of return, which is the historical return for the market.

Market Investments vs. Savings Accounts

Another important factor in the amounts of money the brothers had to draw on when they retired is that they both chose to invest in the market rather than going the more traditional route of making deposits to a savings account in a financial institution.

Investing in the stock market isn't always a better alternative than depositing money in a savings account. Savings accounts are appropriate for short-range goals, like setting money aside for next year's tuition fees, getting some new furniture, or paying cash for a better car. But for long-range goals like retirement or a new home in ten or 20 years, investing is a much better idea. The reason is the difference in interest rates. At the time this book was published in 2020, savings account rates in banks were in the 1.5–1.75% range. Historically, the stock market, on average, has paid about 5% more than savings accounts, and even with the elevator rides the market took in 2020 due to the COVID-19 pandemic, most market observers expect that long-range results will not be much different.

The table below shows the difference between saving and investing after an initial deposit of $50,000 and then adding $1,000 per month for 20 years:

The opportunity cost of not being in the market in the long run is undeniable

$1,077,531

$348,950

Market Return (9.5% annualized)

---Saving (1.5% annualized)

| | 2020 | 2022 | 2024 | 2026 | 2028 | 2029 | 2031 | 2033 | 2035 | 2037 | 2039 | 2040 |

$1,200,000
$1,000,000
$800,000
$600,000
$400,000
$200,000
$0

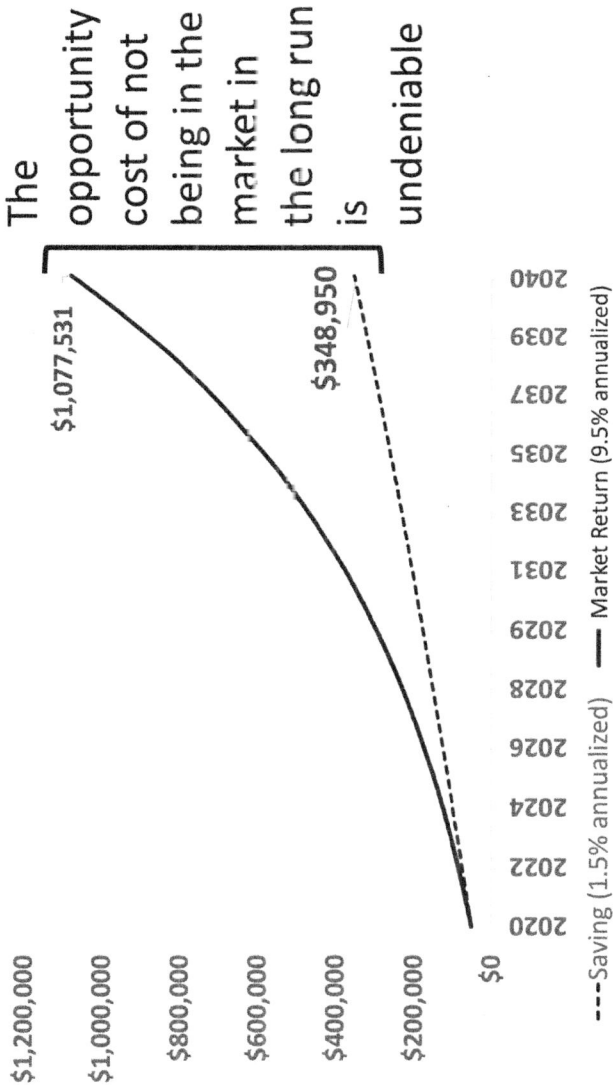

Figure 9: The difference between saving and investing after an initial deposit of $50,000 and then adding $1,000 per month for 20 years. As apparent in this graph, while joining the stock market comes with risk, it also provides superior return opportunities for the investor.

RULE 4

Make the Tax Person Your Friend

"...in this world nothing can be said to be certain, except death and taxes."
—Benjamin Franklin

Income Tax Is Here to Stay

First introduced in the U.S. in 1861 to help finance the Civil War and later enshrined in the Sixteenth Amendment to the United States Constitution (this time, to help finance World War I), income tax has become something that millions of people love to hate. In Canada, income tax was similarly brought in as a temporary measure in 1917 to help fund the First World War, and it has never left.

Federal income tax rates for individuals in the U.S. range from 10–37% (2019). The situation in Canada is a similar: 15–33%. The base 10% applies to U.S. taxpayers earning $9,700, but the bill goes up to 22% when earnings reach $39,476. The bottom Canadian tax bracket (15%) continues to apply until earnings reach $47,630.

State income tax rates and tax laws in the U.S. are determined by each state and vary considerably. In fact, some states, such as Alaska and Florida, have no state income tax at all. Canadian provincial income tax rates are based on a percentage of the federal tax, and deductions and tax rules are the same in all provinces.

One fundamental difference that should be noted between the two countries is that Canadian income tax revenues help pay the costs of a universal health care plan that provides access to medical facilities, procedures, and practitioners with no direct fees charged to the patient. As seen in the budget figures listed in the introduction to this book, Americans typically pay significant out-of-pocket expenses for their health insurance plans or for medical fees directly.

Minimizing Your Taxes

While, as Benjamin Franklin observed in 1789, taxes are one of the only two certainties in life, there are steps that can be taken to reduce how much tax you need to pay.

One of the easiest (and most satisfying) ways is to make some contributions to yourself. This doesn't mean that buying yourself gifts will reduce your taxes, but contributing to your own retirement account can have that effect. Contributions to your 401(k) and individual retirement account (IRA) if you are in the U. S. and to your Registered Retirement Savings Plan (RRSP) if you are in Canada can be deducted from your taxable income and reduce the amount of federal tax you owe. These contributions are tax-free until you retire.

Another U. S. tax-reducing strategy for your own future well-being is a Health Savings Account. Your contributions to this account will provide you with an immediate tax deduction. Contributions are tax-deferred and, when the need arises, you can make tax-free withdrawals for qualified medical expenses. As with a retirement account, any balance that remains at the end of the year can be rolled over indefinitely. Thanks to universal health care in Canada, Canadians do not have to worry about saving for health costs; in addition, medical expenses that Canadians do pay out of pocket (e. g. deductibles for prescriptions and anything else that is not covered) can be deducted from your tax return once it reaches a certain minimum.

Tax-sheltered savings accounts (such as the Roth IRA in the U.S. and the Tax-Free Savings Account — or TFSA — in Canada) exempt investors from paying income tax on accumulating interest. Both allow for investing in a number of options that are more attractive than regular bank savings accounts, such as GICs, stocks, and bonds. Because the income tax has already been paid on the principal amounts and the interest is tax-exempt, there are no taxes due upon withdrawal. As might be expected, there are plenty of limitations and conditions on these government-initiated programs.

Other ways that taxes can be minimized include enrolling in educational programs and, of course, making charitable donations, plus, in Canada but not the U.S., donations to political parties and campaigns.

Business-related Deductions

If you are self-employed, which for many younger people in particular means running a side-hustle, there are a number of business deductions that can reduce how much tax you have to pay. These can include claiming expenses for home office space, office equipment and supplies, business-related vehicle expenses, shipping, advertising, website fees, a percentage of telephone and internet costs, professional publications, professional dues, memberships, and other costs incurred to operate your business. If you pay for your own health, dental, or long-term care insurance, those premiums may be deductible. In the U.S., it is possible to deduct half of your self-employment taxes. If business and pleasure can be carefully combined, even vacation travel can't be ruled out.

The kinds of deductions you can legitimately claim will depend, of course, on the kind of business you're in. Driving your car for Uber is quite different from operating a dog-walking service, and different again from writing and self-publishing your own books and receiving royalties. What is important is to not get carried away by making questionable claims on your tax return. All of us would prefer to make the tax man (now perhaps more appropriately referred to as the "tax person") our friend and not our opponent.

These kinds of deduction possibilities can, of course, lead to abuse, and you can be sure that tax people and the programs they use have already encountered countless examples of this. To resist being misled by temptation and to avoid the penalties that governments are entitled to impose, veteran self-employers have learned to keep careful records of any expenses they plan to claim and especially to retain all relevant receipts, either in their computer files or on paper (shoe boxes have served this purpose for decades).

Another way to avoid the wrath of the tax person is to have your tax returns (business and personal, or, more likely, a combination of the two) prepared by a specialized professional. There are certainly software programs available, but the expertise of an experienced tax preparer might reveal even more ways to minimize your taxes than you are aware of and can help ensure that your return will not be raising bureaucratic eyebrows. And in some situations, the fees charged by a tax preparer are themselves tax-deductible. Just be sure to choose someone who is familiar with and has experience with the tax aspects of your type of business — and that probably excludes the tv-advertised franchises that pop up periodically like toadstools on lawns to occupy empty storefronts in malls. Word of mouth is probably the best way to find a tax preparer who will meet your needs.

Keep in mind that, generally speaking, employees pay the most taxes. You pay far fewer taxes on your investments if you are a registered business or a corporation.

Registering your business, especially as a sole proprietorship or partnership, is a relatively simple and inexpensive process.

Depending on where you live, you can find quite a bit of information about this online, as well as the opportunity to do it yourself. There is, of course, the alternative of forming a corporation, which has additional legal and tax benefits but can be a more costly and complicated process. If you have decided to hire a tax professional to file your income tax, they (or a lawyer) could offer helpful advice on whether or not and how to register your business.

Save Now, Pay the Taxes Later

One way you can reduce the amount of income tax you are required to pay in a given year is to enrol in a tax deferral plan, such as the 401(k) plan in the U.S.A. or the Registered Retirement Savings Plan (RRSP) in Canada. Both are government-initiated plans and offer the opportunity to delay paying income tax on limited amounts of money until sometime in the future. If you wait to withdraw money from these plans until you have retired and your income is lower than it was during your working years, you will probably be in a lower tax bracket and will owe the tax person less than you would have if you had paid the tax around the same time you received the income. That is why these plans are almost always used as a retirement savings strategy.

Both plans allow investment in a diversified mix of options including bonds, stocks, guaranteed investment certificates (GICs), and mutual funds, and many employers contribute to their employees' plans as a way supporting their personal pension funds.

RULE 5

Understand Good Debt and Bad Debt

"Debt on anything that depreciates is disastrous."
—Orrin Woodward

The Dangers and Advantages of Debt

When we were growing up, many of us were taught by our family members and in school that being in debt was a bad thing. We were told that we should put off buying what we wanted until we could pay cash or, in the case of major purchases like a car or certainly a house, to wait until we were able to accumulate a major down payment. We might also have been warned about being tempted by credit cards that made it easy to acquire what we wanted and then charged us astoundingly high rates of interest for years to come.

Although it's easy to criticize the use of consumer credit cards, they can be convenient tools if used properly. The most obviously sensible way to use these cards is to pay the balance in full each month. That way you really don't have to care what their current rates of interest are. Plus, many credit cards come with a variety of perks, including discounts on merchandise, cash-back payments, and the opportunity to accumulate points for air travel, merchandise, and many other goodies. One factor to keep in mind with cards that offer perks is that they usually require payment of an annual fee. Another reason for the responsible use of a credit card or two is that it can form the basis of a positive credit rating.

Like many of the lessons we learned as children, it turns out that reality is not that simple. Not only is debt not necessarily bad, but there is actually such a thing a good debt. Debt can be considered good when it will eventually increase the value of an asset. A possible example of that is taking out a mortgage to buy a house or, even better, a cashflow-generating rental property. Bad debt is taken on to purchase items that don't increase in value over time or, even worse, actually depreciate. A loan on a new (or even used) car is a classic example of bad debt. So is ongoing credit card debt, as well as any other kind of debt with high interest rates, especially if it is for unnecessary or frivolous purchases. And, of course, payday loans are just plain "ugly debt."

Not everyone agrees on how to classify various kinds of debt. Forbes, for instance, considers student loans to be good debt because such loans allow you to complete your education and increase your potential long-term earnings. Other experts say a student loan is a bad debt because it cannot be refinanced or repackaged.

Many financial writers define good debt as debt that will help you generate cashflow and bad debt as debt that sucks up your cashflow. Robert Kiyosaki maintains that good debt is used to buy assets, puts money into your pockets, and makes you rich, while bad debt is used for consumption, takes money out of your pocket, and makes you poor.

Having a mortgage on a rental property, for example, is a good debt because you are using the leverage to generate cashflow for yourself. Good debt can help you limit your taxes because interest comes before taxes on the income statement.

Paying Off Debt

Although allowing a debt to run its full term while making minimum payments is an option, it can be an expensive process. This is notoriously true for credit cards, where interest rates in May 2020 averaged 16% and some crept well into the mid-20s. Using an example of an Aeroplan Visa card that same month, paying off a balance of just over $2,000 by making the mandatory minimum payment of $10 per month would take more than 15 years based on the current annual interest rate of 19.99%. Not too many people are likely to go willingly down that path.

A form of temporary relief for people who find themselves with a credit card balance they want to eliminate is known as a balance transfer. Credit card providers are always looking for new customers, and many are willing to allow holders of their cards to transfer outstanding balances from competitors' cards to their own. This makes sense if the transfer is from a card (or cards) with higher interest rates to one with lower interest rates. There are even occasional special offers to entice balance transfers by charging reduced interest rates (or even a zero-interest rate) for the first few months. But when those honeymoons are over, there is still debt that has to be paid off in one way or another, even if the interest rate is less painful than before.

Two of the most common strategies for paying off debt are known as the snowball method and the avalanche method. The debt snowball method is based on a psychological rationale that is backed by research from Harvard University. It involves eliminating the debt with the smallest balance first and then moving on to the next smallest balance.

The strategy is to pay as much as you possibly can on just one debt (the smallest one at the time) while making minimum payments on all the others. Because you are aiming all of your available financial firepower at that one debt, and because it has a relatively small balance, you should be able to score at least a small psychological victory by paying it off fairly quickly. That victory should make you feel good about yourself and your debt-defeating abilities in general. As the months go by and the momentum builds, you will be receiving fewer bills and especially fewer overdue notices, and you should be feeling increasingly confident about your financial situation. A study reported in the Harvard Business Review indicated that people using the debt snowball method finished paying off their debts more quickly than those using other methods. One mathematical downside, of course, is that all of those months of semi-neglecting the other debts with the biggest balances can add up to paying a lot of interest.

The debt avalanche method is based on mathematical principles and recommends paying off the debts with the highest interest rates first. This approach means that you will end up paying less total interest than you would with the debt snowball strategy, but it might not be as emotionally satisfying.

PART 2

🔑 MANAGING YOUR INCOME

RULE 6

Have Smart Financial Priorities

"Most people don't plan to fail. They fail to plan."
—John L. Beckley

The Waterfall Method

In order to be in a position where you can realistically begin to invest, you first need to put your financial house in order. Or, to use another cliché, you need to clear the decks.

In practical terms, this means taking care of half a dozen preliminary steps that will strengthen your financial position so investing becomes something that you and your financial situation can handle comfortably and with reasonable prospects for success.

The diagram below illustrates what is known as the waterfall method and can be compared to the tiered water fountains often used as a landscaping features or to the "champagne towers" of carefully-stacked wine glasses often seen at social events. With both, the water or champagne is poured onto the artificial waterfall from the top to fill the top tier first. When that level is filled, the liquid overflows to the level beneath it. This goes on until all of the t ers are filled.

In the waterfall approach to financial stability, the approach is similar. The top task (eliminating high-interest debt) needs to be completed before building an emergency fund (the next one down) can begin.

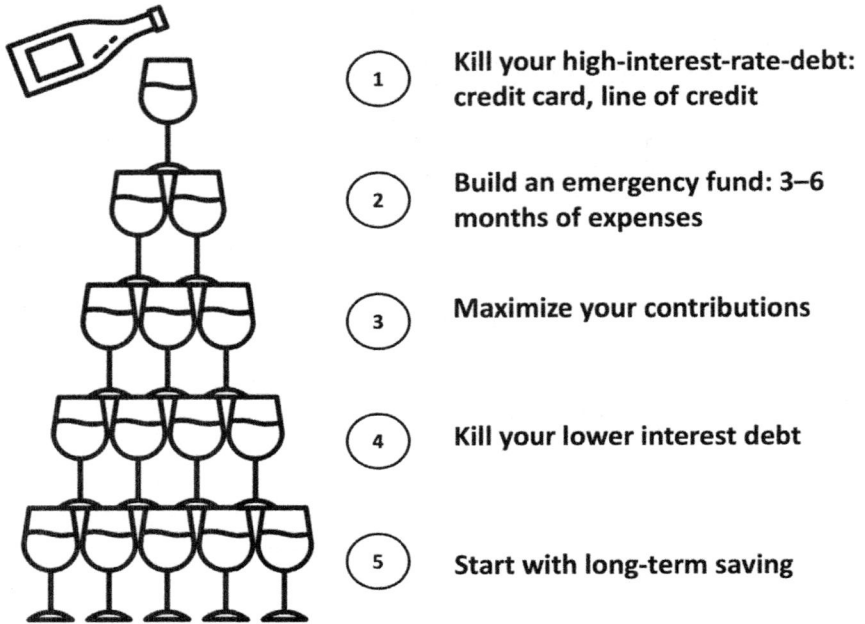

1. **Kill your high-interest-rate-debt: credit card, line of credit**

2. **Build an emergency fund: 3–6 months of expenses**

3. **Maximize your contributions**

4. **Kill your lower interest debt**

5. **Start with long-term saving**

Figure 10: In the waterfall method, you start with the item that is creating the biggest burden on you financially. For most people this is usually their credit card. The high interest charges get most of their cash flow.

Get Rid of High-Interest Debt

Probably the kindest form of high-interest consumer debt that people find themselves saddled with is credit card debt; other high-interest loans and debt, especially "bad debt," can be much more cruel and painful. As mentioned previously, the annual interest rates on credit cards are extremely high, and choosing to make only the minimum payments required by the card issuer can be a long-term and costly albatross around the neck of an unfortunate cardholder. Because those interest rates are probably significantly higher than the rate of return that investments are likely to produce, it only makes mathematical sense to pay off all of your credit card debt before you begin to invest. An added bonus of such a strategy is that your credit rating will probably improve considerably.

Other possible examples of high-interest debt are auto loans, private student loans, and, of course, those payday loans from hell.

Build an Emergency Fund

Everyone needs to have a certain amount of money set aside to deal with emergencies such as accidents, illness, job loss, and unexpected home and vehicle repairs.

Even in countries like Canada where virtually all medical expenses are covered by universal health care plans, there are always incidental costs that may not be taken care of, even by supplemental insurance providers like Blue Cross. Where there are no government plans, and even when regular insurance premiums (as in the U.S.) are included in the household budget, there are deductibles and incidental expenses that have to be met. For people without dental health coverage, paying for a crown or a root canal, for instance, can be a problem.

When we looked at living from paycheck to paycheck in the introduction, we learned of the 39% who would not be able to come up with $3,000 if an emergency arose. It's not difficult to think of possibilities that would cost that much or more: roof and foundation repairs to your house or condo; an illness or accident that finds siblings or very close friends needing a helping hand; veterinary expenses for your loyal pet that are not covered by insurance; going on strike or getting laid off at work; aging parents whose pension income just can't handle all their bills.

Many sources recommend utilizing a no-risk savings account at a bank or credit union with no restrictions on deposits or withdrawals to set aside three months of expenses for singles and six months for families.

Maximize Whatever Your Employer Is Willing to Match

If you're fortunate enough to have an employer that is willing to match your contributions to your retirement fund, don't be shy. That is free money, and it makes no sense to turn it down. Contribute as much as you are allowed and as your discretionary funds can handle.

If you're afraid your employer might eventually shut down or go bankrupt, don't be. Retirement funds are placed in trust accounts that are safe and are not directly connected to your employer.

Get Smart about Taxes

Probably the smartest way to deal with taxes is not to have to pay them. That doesn't mean tax evasion (which is not smart at all). It means finding shelter through them, as in Roth IRAs in the U.S. and TFSAs in Canada, and other strategies we discussed in "Minimizing Your Taxes" in Rule 4.

Get Rid of Low-Interest Debt

Now that you've eliminated your high-interest debt, it's time to eliminate the low-interest counterparts as well. Although long-term obligations like home mortgages, car loans, and student loans might have relatively low interest rates, even those low rates will detract from what you will be earning from your investments. Debt by any other name is still debt.

Set Up Some Personal Goals

After building a strong foundation for eliminating all of your personal debt, setting aside sufficient funds to cover most emergencies, maximizing your pension fund contributions, and minimizing your taxes, you should be ready to set up some personal investment goals. In other words, what is the money you earn from your investments going to buy for you? You might want to set up a personal account for ongoing use or to maximize your pension account for your Golden Years. Perhaps you will want to have some savings for a new car or new house.

RULE 7

Budget Sustainably

> *"Annual income, twenty pounds; annual expenditure, nineteer pounds; result, happiness. Annual income, twenty pounds; annual expenditure, twenty-one pounds; result, misery."*
> **—Charles Dickens**

Budgeting Strategies

There are at least four basic budgeting strategies: reverse budgets, values-based budgets, zero-sum budgets, and percentage budgets. Probably the best approach for most individuals is a blend of the features of each that best match their financial situations and personalities.

- Reverse budgets are often promoted with the enticing slogan "Pay ourself first." and unlike other approaches that begin with figuring out how much needs to be spent, this process begins with determining how much is going to be saved. Th s trickle-down approach can be described as "Save first, then spend the rest." The usual first step is to deposit a predetermined amount from your paycheck (typically 10%) into your savings or investment accounts. In the event of extra income (raises, bonuses, tax refunds, windfalls) the percentage saved or invested should be more like 50%. The second step is paying for essentials, such as housing, food, transportation, utilities, and insurance. The third step is discretionary spending, such as eating out, entertainment, and treating yourself and others to something special.

- Values-based budgeting focuses your spending on what is important to you. It encourages you to determine what matters the most to you and then find ways to channel as much money as possible into paying for those things. This, of course, is a personalized approach, and your priorities will change over time. Because it starts with you and what matters to you, this can be an enjoyable way to budget. It does, however, take time to implement and might not prepare you for the future as well as other approaches. It is similar to zero-sum, but it requires more self-awareness.

- A zero-sum budget actually aims for a balance of zero in your checking account each month. Then the next month begins with a clean slate and a new spending budget. It requires you to "give every dollar a job" as you spend every available dollar on your regular bills, out-of-pocket spending, savings, and investments. Unlike some other budget schemes, each expenditure is regarded as a bill, so investments and savings account deposits are treated the same as credit card bills and mortgage payments.

- Percentage budgets are probably the most popular and most logical kind of budget. Some versions are extremely simple, such as the 50/30/20 approach (50% for needs, 30% for wants, 20% for savings). Others divide the allocations into several categories, and the following is a typical example:

  - 55% for necessities: housing, groceries, transportation, insurance, healthcare

- 🔑 10% for long-term savings (first priority to emergency fund: 6–12 months)

- 🔑 10% for a financial freedom account: investment for passive residual income, such as online businesses, stocks

- 🔑 10% for education seminars, courses, coaches, mentors, books

- 🔑 10% for entertainment and life balance

- 🔑 5% for giving to others

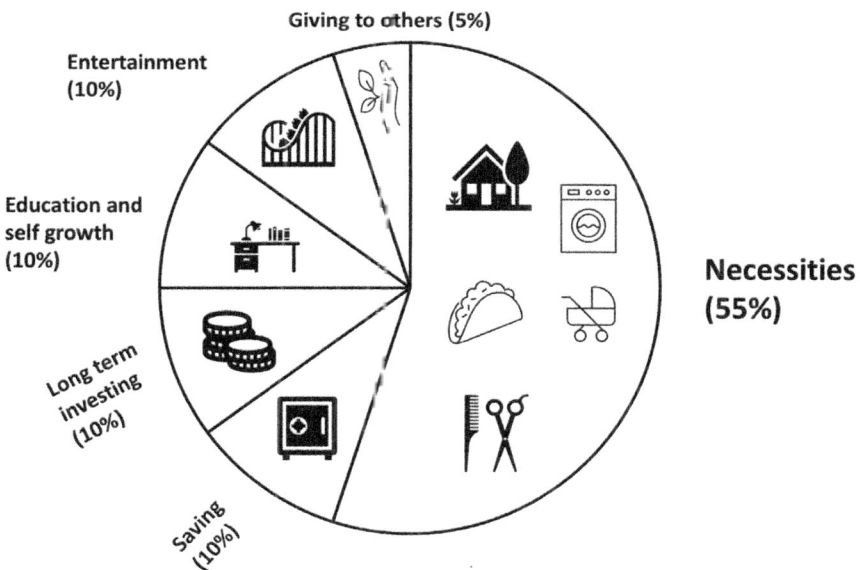

Figure 11: An example of a percentage-based budget. This is one of my favorite approaches, where you do not sacrifice your convenience as much but still allocate enough money for your future and personal development.

Money Management

Money management is one of the most important life skills you can possess, and it might not be something that your parents or your schools taught you.

To begin with, though, you need to have some money to manage. For most people, that means getting a job. If, for some reason, you don't happen to have one at the moment, remember the old saying about beggars and choosers. Maybe you had a bad experience flipping burgers for minimum wage as a teenager and don't want to do that again—ever. Please keep in mind that even minimum wage is more money than no money at all. Or maybe you don't want to do manual labor and get your hands (and maybe the rest of you) dirty. Please remember that some of those jobs pay really well, and you could save lots of money in a short period of time. And you can be looking for a better job in your free time.

In addition, a job, any job, gives you experience and references to add to your resume, which helps you get better jobs with better pay and cleaner hands. Being paid for doing a job enables you to cover your living expenses, go out and do things, and, more importantly, save up money to take some courses and maybe even start your own business.

If you are going to set up a budget and manage your money, you will need an accurate way of keeping track of your income and expenses. Many people have found that a simple Excel spreadsheet works well. There are also plenty of apps available to help you. Some of the most popular ones at the time this book was published were You Need a Budget (YNAB), Mvelopes, Quicken, Mint, CountAbout, Moneydance, Personal Capital, and Acorns. There will be many more coming along. Some are designed to utilize one or more of the budgeting strategies described in the previous section, and, of course, there are online reviews to help you choose one that will work for you. Keep in mind that monthly and yearly figures are useful in long-range terms, but if you really want to keep track of your money in the most helpful ways, be sure to monitor weekly figures as well.

Rationalizing Your Expenses

One of the most effective ways to take full advantage of your earnings is to mentally step back and take a really hard look at your spending. Let's take another look at the average American income and expenditure figures listed at the beginning of the introduction to this book:

According to the U.S. Bureau of Labor Statistics, consumers in 2018 made $67,421 annually after taxes on average and spent $61,224. That spending worked out to $5,102 each month for the average American household. It broke down as follows:

- 32. 8% ($1,674) for housing

- 15.9% ($813) for transportation (including public transit, lease or loans payments, fuel and servicing)

- 11.9% ($608) for personal insurance and pensions

- 8.1% ($414) for health care

- 7.3% ($372) for groceries

- 5.6% ($288) for restaurants

- 5.3% ($269) for entertainment

Now let's do some brainstorming on some potential ways these expenditures can be reduced. Of course, downsizing means making some sacrifices, but the ultimate goal for this kind of short-term discomfort is to create wealth as a way to achieve financial freedom.

Housing: Move back to (or don't leave) your parents' home for another couple of years. Of course, you probably wouldn't enjoy living in your childhood bedroom or the basement and it would not be a way to impress your friends, but think of the money you could save or invest, even after paying a reasonable amount for room and board. An alternative would be to move in with one or more friends (or invite them to move in with you) and come to an agreement on sharing expenses. Your parents' home is probably a better idea though—it comes with less chance of you hosting parties or going out to bars. For your own psychological and social well-being, come to an agreement with everyone involved (including yourself) on the terms and length of these temporary living arrangements. Otherwise, at age 32 and living in your mother's basement, you could find yourself the subject of a television series.

If you own a home, sign up with Airbnb and rent out rooms.

If you are renting, consider moving to something less expensive. And make sure it's really close to your job and shopping or close to public transportation, because then you won't need your money-sucking car.

Transportation: If are living close to your job, shopping, and transit, you can enjoy a car-free life. You can walk, cycle, or take transit to work. If you live close to places where you can shop (especially for groceries), you can walk there and back. If you do that fairly often, you can carry what you buy. For larger purchases, utilize the grocery carts and folding wagons available at Walmart, COSTCO, and other places. For trips to COSTCO, consider transit to get there and Uber or Lyft to haul your shopping home. While you're taking all these car-free trips, think about the money you're now able to save or invest and the health benefits of walking and cycling.

If you really do need a car, look at used or certified pre-owned. Check online and in Consumer Reports for which makes and models best hold their value over time. Pay cash if possible, and avoid long-term and high-interest loans.

Groceries: You can save money on groceries if you always use a list (from which you should not deviate) and never go when you're hungry (to prevent impulse purchases). Planning menus for the next few days and buying the needed ingredients in appropriate quantities can minimize spoilage, waste, and overeating. Checking store ads and stocking up on staples like cleaning supplies, paper items, and non-perishables when they are on sale is a wise strategy. Not so wise is becoming a hoarder and being featured on a different television series.

Although COSTCO savings on a range of items are legend, paying for even a basic membership for a household of one or two might offset a lot of those savings. Making an occasional trip to COSTCO with someone you know who has a membership (and a vehicle) is a much better idea. If you are thinking of a trip to CCSTCO, keep in mind that their competitors sometimes have sale prices that are just as low as COSTCO and in smaller sizes.

Steer clear of those humongous COSTCO-size items if you're not positive you can use them up completely, or split the purchase with a friend or relative. Household items like bathroom tissue, paper towels, and facial tissue can be good buys, especially when they are on sale, as long as you have storage space for them. However, perishable food items in large quantities can turn out to be unwise purchases if you can't finish them before their expiry date or if you just get tired of eating them.

Restaurants: It's worth noting in the Bureau of Labor Statistics survey that grocery spending ($372) and restaurant spending ($288) are not all that far apart. If eating restaurant food, including takeout and delivery, becomes more of a special treat and less of a regular event, your grocery bills might go up somewhat, but there will still be budget savings that can be invested.

Entertainment: If you're a movie fan, keep in mind that most theater operators have special prices on certain days of the week or at certain times (e. g. matinées). Discount deals for admissions and snacks are sold in some retail outlets.

It might be a good idea to rethink your cable TV selections. How many of those channels do you really watch? Cutting back to only the basic channels can reduce your cable bill significantly. How about cutting the cord completely? There are increasing alternatives to cable, such as over-the-air broadcasts and various internet opportunities that are rapidly changing and expanding.

If you are into Netflix and similar streaming services, where the selection of movies, series programming, and documentaries is rapidly outpacing traditional television, consider signing up for only the basic option. Of course, basic YouTube is free, at least for now, and can be entertaining.

RULE 8

Automate Your Finances 🔑

*"Any sufficiently advanced technology
is indistinguishable from magic."*
—Arthur C. Clarke

Fintech Is Your Friend

Financial technology, "fintech" for short, refers to computer programs and other kinds of technology used to support or enable banking and financial services. It has been described as one of the fastest growing areas for venture capitalists.

When the concept of fintech emerged around the year 2000, the term was applied to technology used by financial institutions. Since then, the definition has expanded into consumer-oriented services. Fintech now encompasses a wide range of organizations and industries, including education, retail banking, non-profits, and investment management. Examples are constantly expanding and can range from electronic money transfers to depositing checks from smartphones to managing investments. The key factor is that these are financial activities that are generally carried out without the assistance of a person.

Automated Investing

One of the countless examples of fintech is automated investing. Two of the most common methods that are utilized are the overflow method and the roundup method.

The overflow method automatically transfers surplus funds into your low-interest or no-interest checking account to investment accounts or high-interest saving accounts.

The roundup method gathers up your transactions and invests them for you with low management fees. There are many apps for that, including Mylo, Wealthsimple, MoneyFarm, iQuant, Nutmeg, and Axos Invest.

Out of Sight, Out of Mind

Most paychecks are automatically deposited to employees' checking accounts in the bank or other financial institution of their choice. If yours isn't, it would be a good idea to see if your employer offers this option.

Regardless of how your pay makes its way into your checking account, it shouldn't be left to suffer in that interest-starved environment for long. That is something your friendly banker should be happy to help you with. If they're not, it's time to shop around.

The following diagram illustrates how the concept can work:

Automate your finances

Before your income hits your account

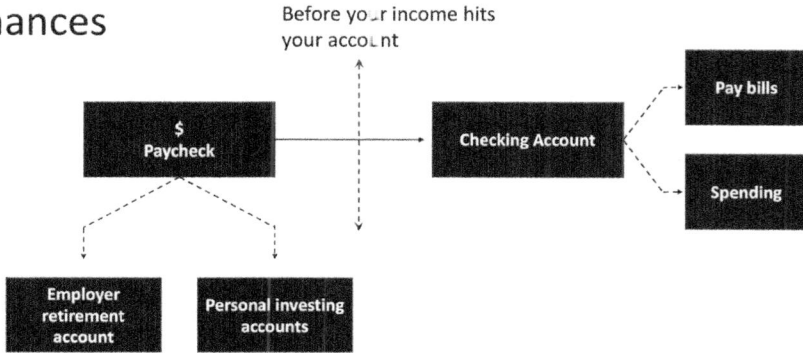

Figure 12: Automating your finances is one of the keyways you can save and invest. You should set the process up so that part of your income gets invested before your paycheck hits your bank account.

Before your paycheck deposit gets too comfortable in its new and unproductive checking account home, your bank's technology will instantly, through an automatic recurring transfer process, move whatever percentage or fixed amount you've prearranged to your employer's retirement account, where it will hopefully be matched in some fashion and tax-sheltered in some way.

The other two priorities are saving and investing, and again, an automatic recurring transfer each pay period will move your funds for you. Many banks are also able to arrange recurring transfers for paying credit card balances (hopefully right down to zero) and other kinds of monthly bills, such as electricity, cable, and internet.

The biggest advantages to all of this are that you don't have to lift a finger to make these transactions happen and, maybe even more importantly for many of us, you never see the money and become tempted to spend it in other ways. Because it's out of sight and out of mind, you probably won't even miss it.

PART 3

🔑 INVESTING YOUR INCOME

RULE 9

Invest in Stocks that Pay Dividends

"Buy not on optimism, but on arithmetic."
—Benjamin Graham

As you saw in the first few pages of the book in Figure 3, the stock market has been able to provide some of the best returns in the past 100 years, so it would be foolish to write a book on financial literacy and freedom and not talk about the market. The reason for stock market growth is actually quite simple. When you invest in the U.S. equity market, you are betting on one of the greatest economies in the world. As long as the earning prospects of the companies you have invested in are growing, their stock must go up as well. In the past 100 years, the stock market has provided an average return of 9%, with half of this return coming from earning growth and the other half coming from the dividends companies have paid. The graph below shows the S&P 500 Index return over the past 100 years.

S&P 500 Index return over the past 100 years

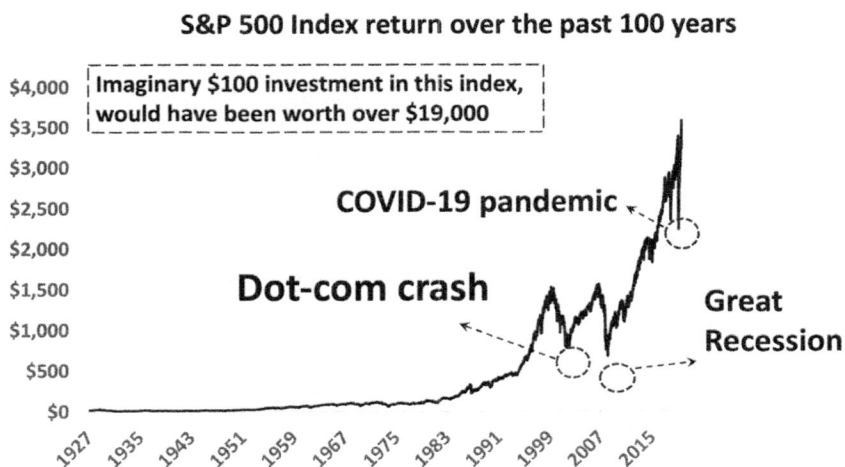

Figure 13: An imaginary $100 investment 100 years ago would have been worth over $19,000 today. That is an average annual return of 9.5%. Of course, there would have been years such as the dot com crash, the Great Recession, and the recent 2020 pandemic, when the market has had negative returns.

While a graph from the past could be misleading at times, it is a good indicator of the overall market. These types of charts can present an appealing picture of investing in stocks, but entering the stock market is not an easy task for an average Joe or Jane. Which companies to invest in, which broker to use, how much commission to pay, and many other questions can make breaking into the stock market a daunting task. In addition, Wall Street bankers purposefully use a great deal of specific lingo to make it look like they are the only people that can do what they do. They love to over-complicate processes and charge obscene management fees in order to finance their lifestyle.

In my first book. Stock Market Explained: A Beginner's Guide to Investing and Trading in the Modern Stock Market, I go into detail on how to pick winning stocks, how to read charts, and how to select companies in different sectors based on fundamental and technical analysis. This information is beyond the scope of this book, and if you are interested in learning more, please feel free to view my other book, or send me an email at Ardi@peakcapital-trading.com. I always enjoy receiving email from curious learners, and it is a pleasure to connect with you.

For this book, I review two key concepts when it comes to the stock market: the difference between value and growth stock, and how to generate income from dividend stocks. By no means will this section will make you a wizard in the market, but it is an introduction for you to know where to start.

Value Stocks vs. Growth Stocks

Investors who are interested in stocks will find that there are two basic types: value stocks and growth stocks. Value stocks can be defined as stocks that are currently trading below the intrinsic value of the company. These may be companies that have become less appealing to investors but still have good fundamentals, or new companies that have not yet been recognized by investors.

These are the stocks that pay dividends, and 70% of stock market returns come from dividends. These are the kinds of stocks I recommend. But it is not just me who recommends stocks that pay dividends. Even Kevin O'Leary, founder of O'Leary Funds Inc. and an investor on ABC's hit TV show, Shark Tank, agrees with me. Kevin occasionally quotes the advice his mother gave him when he was young, "Never buy a stock that doesn't pay a dividend." The logic behind O'Leary's thinking (and his mother's) and many other investors is simple. O'Leary puts it this way, "70 percent of the time all the return comes from dividends. Yahoo never paid a dividend. It's never made money for anyone except all the CEO's." There are numerous companies that do not pay dividends and grow in value, but in many cases, they will lose all of their value before making you (the investor) any money.

When looking into value stocks, investors typically research the fundamentals of the business to assess the value of the company.

If the market price appears to be below what the investor considers to be the value of the company, they decide that the stock is undervalued and conclude that it is a value stock.

The market prices of stocks are set by stock exchanges, based on the prices that investors are offering and bidding. This means that a prospective investor can easily determine the price of a stock simply by looking at the last traded price in that stock.

Determining the intrinsic value of a company is a much more subjective process. When investors look at such factors as the net assets a company controls and its future market place prospects, their judgment will be heavily influenced by their own views on business and investing. In other words, different investors can come to very different conclusions on the value of the same company.

Value stocks trade at prices that appear to be low in comparison to the estimated true value of the stocks, or to similar stocks, and are often viewed as bargains. Investors often buy them in the hope their prices will appreciate when the market eventually recognizes the real value of the company.

Some value stocks have come about as a result of investor overreaction to company problems such as disappointing earnings, negative publicity, legal problems, or other factors that have created doubt about the company's long-term prospects.

Value stocks tend to move up and down with global economic cycles. They also generally have a long-term history of growing revenue and earnings per share, have low debt, and are known for increasing their dividends.

Growth stocks can be described as companies that are expected to grow more quickly than the average growth for the market. Their investors are willing to pay high price-to-earnings multiples because they expect to be able to sell them at even higher prices as the companies continue to grow.

These stocks do not pay dividends because they need all the cash they make from their operation to fund their growth.

Growth stocks exhibit rapid earnings or revenue growth rates compared with similar stocks and generally trade at high prices in comparison to the market in general. Investors purchase growth stocks with hopes of seeing continuing growth and rapid appreciation in their stock prices.

It should be kept in mind, however, that rapid growth brings increased volatility. Growth stock investors have to be willing to live with roller-coaster rides with their stocks and need to have a high level of risk tolerance.

Value or Growth: What is Best for You?

There is an ongoing debate between professionals in the market on where to invest your money. Some say the value is the best strategy, and some swear by growth. The truth, however, is that the research is unclear, and when you look at historical returns, there are times where value perform better than growth and vice versa. Looking at the past 14 years, you can see value performed better in the latter half of the 2000s while growth dominated the 2010s.

Figure 14: A quick comparison of Vanguard Value (VTV) vs Vanguard Growth (VUG) E.T.F. As you can see, from 2004–2010, Value was performing better than Growth, but in the past 10 years Growth has dominated Value in terms of returns. It is worth noting, however, that value stocks in general pay quarterly dividends, which, in return, could be reinvested or used to purchase other assets. While I typically do not deeply believe in the value vs growth argument, I think the most important thing before entering the market is to set an investment philosophy.

What is Investment Philosophy, and Why is it Important?

Regardless of what you believe about value funds, growth funds, or dividends, the most important thing before investing your money is to have a fund philosophy. What do I mean by that? I mean coming up with a structure that you cherish and sticking by it. As an example, I follow a 40/20/10/30 approach.

40% of my personal portfolio is invested in value stocks. These are the stocks that I believe are mispriced (underpriced) by the market and have potential to outperform in the next few years as the market and analysts catch up with this stock. This 40% also provides me with a quarterly dividend, which I use either to rein-vest or buy other assets as I see fit.

20% of my portfolio is growth stocks. These are companies that are not yet profitable, but I believe in their business model and their future growth potential. These companies are usually disrupters, like how Uber is to transportation or Airbnb is to the hotel industry. I know there is a high chance these companies may never become profitable or will drop in value significantly (just go look up Blue Apron stock!!). This a risk I take and accept because I know the five to 10-year growth potential of these stocks outweighs the risk.

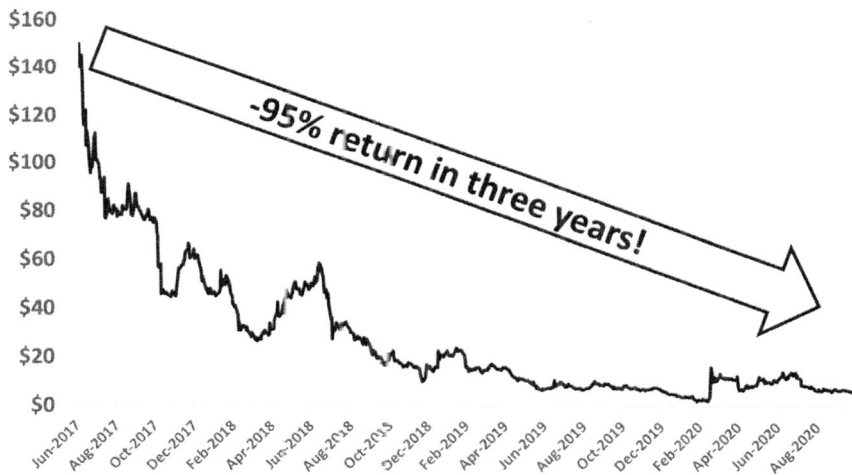

Figure 15: Blue Apron (ticker: APRN) went public in 2017, and many were optimistic about the future of this company and its potential! As you can see, the stock never recorded a higher price than the initial public offering. If you would have invested $100,000 in 2017 for the Blue Apron IPO, your investment would now be worth only $4,193! That is an astonishing -95% rate of return!

Another 10% of my portfolio is designated for brand new IPO listings. To me, these companies, if selected on time and with research, provide the highest rate of return. A prime example of that is Shopify, the Canadian tech powerhouse which operates in software as a service, helping online retailers. A $50,000 invest-ment in this stock in 2016 would have accumulated to $1 million just four years later in 2020.

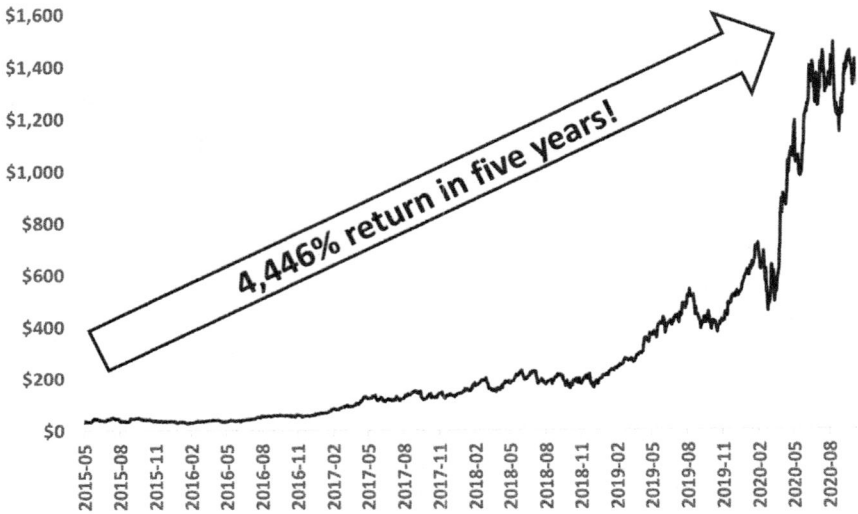

Figure 16: Shopify (ticker: Shop) value since its IPO in 2015! Whoever trusted this company, their management, and their technology would have made a lot of money for themselves.

The other 30% of my portfolio is devoted to bonds and short-term treasury bills, which are risk-free, and their return is enough to beat inflation. This 30% is my safe haven so to speak; I use it to buy stocks if there is a really good opportunity, or I just keep it in a short-term treasury bill.

This is my investment philosophy, and while it has worked great for me over the years and made me a lot of money, it does not have to be yours. You can create your own allocation based on your risk tolerance and beliefs. If you are intrigued by my ideas and explanation of investing, please look at my other book, *Stock Market Explained: A Beginner's Guide to Investing and Trading in the Modern Stock Market.* In that book, I go into more detail on how a lot of these strategies actually work.

While I understand every individual will come up with their own version of investment philosophy and allocate their money accordingly, I cannot emphasize enough how important the dividend stocks are. Just know that more than half the return of the stock market has come from dividend payments, and if you miss out on these stocks, you are osing out on huge opportunities for growth in your portfolio. In the next section, I share with you some of my favorite dividend-paying stocks.

Dividend Yields and Where to Find Them

A dividend yield, which is displayed as a percentage, is the amount of money a company pays shareholders for owning a share of its stock divided by its current stock price. Here is the formula:

dividend yield = annual dividends ÷ per share price

Another way of describing dividend yield is that it is an estimate of the dividend-only return of a stock investment. If the dividend remains the same as before, the yield will rise when the price of the stock falls, and it will fall when the price of the stock rises. Because a dividend yield changes in accordance with the stock price, it can often look unusua y high for stocks that are falling in value quickly.

Well-established companies are the most likely to pay dividends, while utility companies and some consumer firms tend to have higher dividend yields. Real estate investment trusts (REITs), master limited partnerships (MLPs), and business development companies (BDCs) generally pay above-average dividends; however, the dividends from these companies are taxed at a higher rate. Some financial institutions, notably Canadian banks, also pay high dividends.

Because the dividend yield of a stock may be elevated as a result of a declining stock price, higher dividend yields do not necessarily indicate attractive investment opportunities.

Here is a list of 25 high-dividend stocks in the U. S. as of May 2020. The dividends listed are the amounts paid per period and not annually. This list is included for information only, and investment decisions should be made only after due diligence.

Symbol	Company name	Dividend	Dividend yield
NHI	National Health Investors Inc. (REIT)	$1.10	9.27%
MO	Altria Group Inc.	$0.84	9.27%
UVV	Universal Corp.	$0.76	7.34%
CM	Canadian Imperial Bank of Commerce	$1.46	7.32%
BNS	The Bank of Nova Scotia	$0.90	7.08%
BMO	Bank of Montreal	$1.06	6.76%
PFG	Principal Financial Group Inc.	$0.56	6.66%
CVX	Chevron Corp.	$1.29	5.73%
TD	The Toronto-Dominion Bank	$0.79	5.73%
STX	Seagate Technology Plc	$0.65	5.41%
OMC	Omnicom Group Inc.	$0.65	5.18%
BXP	Boston Properties Inc. (REIT)	$0.98	5.11%
EVBN	Evans Bancorp Inc.	$0.58	5.02%
ALE	ALLETE Inc.	$0.62	4.94%
SLF	Sun Life Financial Inc.	$0.55	4.86%
MTB	M&T Bank Corp.	$1.10	4.76%
GPC	Genuine Parts Co.	$0.79	4.45%
WHR	Whirlpool Corp.	$1.20	4.45%

Please look at the above list as just an example of some companies that pay dividends and not as investment advice. Many of the Canadian banks are under pressure due to the low interest rate environment and are more levered (in debt) than their U.S. counterparts. Just because a company has a high dividend yield does not mean it is a good investment. You must do your own research and due diligence before you invest. If you are looking for some advice or suggestions please feel free to email me at Ardi@peakcapitaltrading.com and I will try to get back to you within a few days.

RULE 10

Invest in Real Estate

"But land is land, and it's safer than the stocks and bonds of Wall Street swindlers."
—Eugene O'Neill

Compared to many other investment strategies, investment in real estate can be both profitable and personally gratifying. However, it generally involves a larger financial commitment and can be much more time-consuming. There are a number of different approaches to investment in real property, and they range from direct (literally hands-on) involvement to more indirect strategies. A few of the most common approaches to real estate investment are described below.

Renting Out Space in Your Current Home

Some investors already own a home and are considering the rental market, but they don't want any kind of long-term commitment yet. Renting out a room through sites like Airbnb is a good way to start. Most Airbnb rentals are three days, the average is 4.3 nights, and longer (12-night) rentals comprise only 5% of the total.

The risks are relatively low — you will just be taking in short-term tenants, potential renters undergo a certain amount of pre-screening by Airbnb, and the company's Host Guarantee gives you some protection against damages. Sharing your home with one or more total strangers for a few days should give you some idea of how direct an approach to real estate investment you're comfortable with. How much do you value your privacy? How would you feel about sharing your bathroom (if you have only one) with someone you really don't know? How tolerant are you of people from cultures different from your own who might have a limited command of the only language you speak? Are you as friendly and hospitable as you think you are, especially when the stranger under your roof turns out to have a major personal hygiene problem or expresses viewpoints that you find unacceptable? Will you find yourself counting the hours until they leave or feeling glad that you have found a new friend?

Investing in Rental Properties

A much more long-term approach is to actually go out and buy a rental property. Locating a property that suits your needs, aspirations, and budget is a process that should not be rushed. Most communities have online realtors' listings, and buy-and-sell services like Craigslist have postings for private sales as well as properties that have real estate agents involved. Although logic would suggest that prices for private sales should be lower (no commission!), that isn't necessarily the case. Experienced realtors can point out features of a home (both good and bad) that you and I might not notice, and they generally have a pretty good idea of prices for comparable homes that have recently been sold in the same neighborhood. The best way to find the kind of realtor you want is to ask people you know who have recently bought or sold a home. Is there a house in your neighborhood with a sold sign? Knock on their door and ask them about their real estate agent. Is there a house in your neighborhood that's had a for sale sign for months and months? Knock on their door and ask them about their real estate agent.

Buying a home without first hiring a qualified home inspector is inviting trouble. The fee you pay for an inspection will likely be much less than foundation repairs, roof replacement, or the dozens of other costly issues that can unexpectedly surface in a previously-occupied home. Again, ask other people for recommendations.

You should have a really clear idea of the size and type of home you want and, of course, its location, location, location. If you think you've found just the right home for you, ask for a second showing, and take along some friends or relatives to see if they agree. Before things get serious, co some online browsing at banks and other financial institutions to compare interest rates, and look into getting pre-approved for your mortgage. Incidentally, don't just look at banks. Credit unions are co-operatives, owned by the people they serve. They generally have a more flexible commun ty-centered approach than banks and sometimes better rates.

Unlike stock and bond investors, prospective real estate owners can use leverage to buy a property by paying a portion of the total cost up front, then paying off the balance with interest over time. Leverage enables rental properties to provide regular cashflow while maximizing available capital. Leverage is an investment strategy of using borrowed money to increase the potential return of an investment, but unless you're familiar and hopefully experienced with this process, I suggest you consult a financial advisor.

You obviously need to be quite confident that all of the expenses your rental property will incur are lower than all of the rent you will collect, and your budget should anticipate months when the property is vacant as well as the costs of both routine and unexpected maintenance.

Depending on how much capital, time, and effort you're willing to invest, you might consider anything from a house or condo that you don't plan to live in yourself to a larger home, duplex, or even an apartment building that you might want to rent out entirely or use partly as your own home, a practice known as "house hacking."

If you were to buy a house with multiple bedrooms and bathrooms for instance, you could keep one of each for your own use and rent out the rest. If it's located close to a college or university, the place is clean and comfortable, and the price is reasonable, you could have the ideal setup for students.

One of the advantages of house hacking is that you are living onsite and can see if your property is being treated with respect. You can also take care of maintenance and caretaking issues as soon as they occur. One of the disadvantages is that you are living onsite and could encounter the kinds of problems mentioned earlier regarding Airbnb guests, and this is for a lot more than a few days.

If you are looking ahead to selling your rental and realizing a profit on the sale somewhere down the line, keep in mind that whether or not it is your principal residence could determine if the resulting capital gain is subject to taxation.

When finding, screening, and signing leases with tenants, the paramount rule is the same one that porcupines always observe when making love — it must be done very carefully. States and provinces have specific laws and regulations covering the whole range of residential rentals, from advertising to interviewing to leasing procedures. Many have various forms, often available online, that must be used, and they mandate compulsory deadlines for lease renewals and terminations. Then, of course, there are human rights regulations that forbid discrimination in various ways. If you are considering renting out your property in any way and are not absolutely sure how to do it correctly, I strongly suggest you check the websites of government offices that are responsible for residential rentals and, if you have any doubts, contact them and ask for advice and direction.

Depending on the size of your rental and your own experience, you might want to consider contracting with a property management firm to look after everything from screening tenants and arranging leases to rent collect on and maintenance. Their fees would definitely cut into your revenue, but the time and head-aches you save might be worth it. If you decide to go it alone, be sure to have contingency plans for dealing with home repairs and maintenance. If you aren't confident about your DIY skills or don't have the tools, do some research and have someone lined up to deal with problems as they arise.

Property Flipping

Also known as real estate trading, property flipping has become a household (please pardon the pun) term over the last few years for viewers of HGTV and other reality show channels. It looks really easy on television. Just find an underpriced and somewhat neglected home that needs some love, minor renovations, and redecorating. Give it those things as impressively yet inexpen-sively as possible. Then resell t for a handsome profit and find another home that needs you.

Some property flippers don't look for properties that need work. Their goal is to find a property that is already quite presentable, live in it or rent it out for a while until market prices go up, then sell it for a profit. This technique can work well, but the flipper (and their family) must not mind moving quite often and perhaps on short notice. And if they don't have enough uncommitted cash on hand to pay the mortgage on the unsold property for an ex-tended period of time, they could be facing snowballing losses.

Successful real estate trading requires accurate knowledge of the market and a certain amount of luck. Hot markets can unexpect-edly cool down and result in losses for short-term owners. Unlike buy-and-rent landlords, many flippers try to sell their properties as soon as the updates are completed, typically within six months.

House flipping can be very profitable for people with knowledge of real estate valuation and marketing and expertise in renovations. If that doesn't describe you but you have the capital to invest, try to partner up with someone who does have that knowledge and expertise.

Keep in mind that the longer you hang onto the property, the less money you'll make because you're paying a mortgage on a property that isn't generating any income. If the work that needs to be done is mainly cosmetic and not too messy, you could actually live in the house until it is finished and resold. Also, making it your principal residence could help your tax situation.

Real Estate Investment Products

After considering the time, costs, and risks involved with owning a property as an investment, you may decide to invest in real estate through funds, trusts, and other investment products that provide involvement in the real estate market without actually managing and maintaining properties yourself. This is much more of a hands-off approach.

Several examples of this remote-control approach to property investment are discussed in the following sections.

Real Estate Investment Trusts (REITs)

Real estate investment trusts (REITs) are basically dividend-paying stocks that enable you to invest in real estate without owning or having to look after any actual property. Often compared to mutual funds, REITs are companies that own commercial real estate such as office buildings, retail spaces, apartments, and hotels. REITs tend to pay high dividends, making them desirable retirement investments. Investors who don't need or want the regular income can automatically reinvest those dividends to further increase the value of their investment.

REITs generally do not develop real estate properties to resell, but instead purchase properties to own and often operate. Investment in a REIT enables you to receive income through payouts that the trust receives from the properties that it owns. There are both pub-lic and private REITs.

Public REITs are listed on exchanges, so buying and selling shares in a public REIT is basical y the same as purchasing shares in any other publicly-traded compa ny, and a REIT's share value can eas-ily be determined by checking the price posted on the exchange. You can also learn more about the risks and fees associated with a publicly-traded REIT by reviewing its prospectus. REITs can be purchased through investment brokers.

Private REITs are not listed on exchanges. In Canada, they are sold on the exempt market. n the U.S., private REITs are not sub-ject to most SEC (Securities and Exchange Commission) regulato-ry requirements and are generally sold by brokers to accredited and institutional investors. Because they are significantly riskier investments than public REITs, I recommend that you avoid them.

A corporation is required to pay out 90% of its taxable profits in the form of dividends to retain its REIT status. In this way, REITs avoid paying corporate income tax. A regular company, on the other hand, would first be taxed on its profits and then have to de-cide whether or not to distribute its after-tax profits as dividends.

Like regular dividend-paying stocks, REITs are a reliable investment for stock market investors who are looking for regular cashflow. REITs open doors for ind vic ual investors to be involved in non-res-idential investments, such as malls or office buildings, which are usually not something they can purchase directly. REITs are highly liquid because they are exchange-traded, so you won't need a realtor and a title transfer to help you cash out your investment.

There are some cautions to keep in mind regarding REITs. Because their profits result from renting out the properties they own, they are heavily dependent on having tenants to occupy their properties and pay rent. If any of their buildings have significant vacancies over an extended period of time, the REIT's profitability will be reduced and so will the income paid out to investors.

REITs typically do not perform well when interest rates rise because demand for REITs can drop, reducing the value of any shares that you have. This could mean having to hang on to your investment for longer than originally expected.

Real Estate Investment Groups (REIGs), Real Estate Limited Partnerships (RELPs), Real Estate Investing Platforms, Mortgage Investment Entities (MIEs), Syndicated Mortgages, and Other Non-REIT Schemes

Although there is a certain degree of risk associated with REITs, they are generally regarded as an acceptable and relatively conventional approach to group real estate investment. There are numerous versions of other real estate investment schemes, however, that do not inspire the same level of confidence in the marketplace as REITs. Some of these are listed in the heading to this section, but they can go by an unlimited number of names.

In a nutshell, the best advice I can give to anyone who is not a knowledgeable and experienced investor is to steer clear of such schemes. Whatever it might be called, a risky deal by any other name is still a risky deal and, although tempting, definitely not the way to achieve financial independence.

CONCLUSION

SUMMING IT UP

It has been my pleasure to share with you these ten rules for achieving financial independence. This is, of course, not a definitive list, and your own experiences in the financial world might have taught you rules that are quite different from mine. I hope that you, in turn, will share them with me. I really enjoy helping people to reach their financial goals and to learn new things. This is why I use some of my free time writing articles and sharing the knowledge I have been able to accumulate. I purposely priced this book as low as possible in order to reach as many people as possible. In my opinion, everything I discussed in this book should be taught in school, but unfortunately, in the world in which we live, this is not always the case. Many major organizations profit from our ignorance. The health care industry profits from our ignorance about healthy diets. The wealth management industry profits from our ignorance about the stock market. It almost seems like everyone's main goal is to make money from our lack of knowledge.

I wanted to take the opposite route in this book and provide information at a very economical price. If you have found the topics discussed in this book helpful, please rate and review my book on Amazon. Honest reviews like yours help others to make better-informed decisions. If you believe there are things I could have done better, please send me an email and share your thoughts with me. By now you might even know my email by heart!

As I mentioned in the introduction, I'm looking forward to hearing from you with questions, comments, criticisms, and suggestions about this book. And hopefully you will pass on to me your ideas for more books that could make this the first in an ongoing series.

Finally, just to refresh our collective memories, here are the ten rules on which I based this book:

Rule 1: Master the Income Trilogy.

Rule 2: Distinguish between Assets and Liabilities.

Rule 3: Harness the Power of Compounding.

Rule 4: Make the Tax Person Your Friend.

Rule 5: Understand Good Debt and Bad Debt.

Rule 6: Have Smart Financial Priorities.

Rule 7: Budget Sustainably.

Rule 8: Automate Your Finances.

Rule 9: Invest in Stocks That Pay Dividends.

Rule 10: Invest in Real Estate.

I wish you success in this road to financial freedom and financial literacy. Please remember that financial freedom does not mean living by the beach and working only a few hours each day. Financial freedom is an ongoing journey, a way of life, a constant learning process, and the ability to become smart with money. I am glad to be able to play a small part in your journey towards financial freedom.

ABOUT THE AUTHOR

Ardi Aaziznia is an investment analyst at Peak Capital Trading with multiple years of experience in the capital markets. At Peak Capital Trading, Ardi is responsible for managing firm's portfolio and capital growth with a focused on emerging technologies. Before joining Peak Capital Trading, Ardi was an associate at a private wealth management, helping manage over $200 million dollars in both equity and bond markets. Prior to that, Ardi acted as an investment analyst for a family office in Vancouver, helping managing partners with investment decisions on an array of deal flows.

Ardi is a cum laude alumni of the Sauder School of Business, at University of British Columbia, Vancouver.

When not in the office working with charts and numbers, Ardi can be found reading finance related books, hiking beautiful mountains of British Columbia, or kayaking the Pacific Ocean. Ardi is a firm believer in continuous learning and believes in the power of community and open-source learning. You can email him if you have questions or want to bounce off an investment idea with him (his email is provided in the book).

"People who think they know all the answers, probably don't even know the question."—**Sir John Templeton,** Founder of the Templeton Growth Fund

Printed in Great Britain
by Amazon